AFFIRMATIONS ARE POSI████████████ ███ THAT CAN HELP YOU TO CHAL████████ ████████OME THE SELF-SABOTAGING AND NEGATIVE THOUGHTS THAT CAN SO EASILY ARISE IN A CAREGIVING PROFESSION. WHEN YOU REPEAT THEM OFTEN, AND BELIEVE IN THEM, YOU CAN START TO MAKE POSITIVE CHANGES TO YOUR DAILY LIFE AND FILL YOUR EMOTIONAL CUP.
THE POWER OF POSITIVE AFFIRMATIONS LIES IN REPEATING THEM TO YOURSELF REGULARLY. THIS CAN BE DONE EITHER OUT LOUD OR IN YOUR HEAD. YOU CAN DO THIS FOR A FEW MINUTES EACH MORNING, OR WHEN YOU FEEL THOSE NEGATIVE THOUGHTS OR BEHAVIOURS TAKING HOLD.
GIVEN TIME AND CONSISTENCY, YOU WILL BEGIN TO SEE A HAPPIER, WISER, MORE POSITIVE VERSION OF YOU EMERGING.
BE KIND TO YOURSELF - YOU DESERVE IT!

My smile makes
my patients'
day better

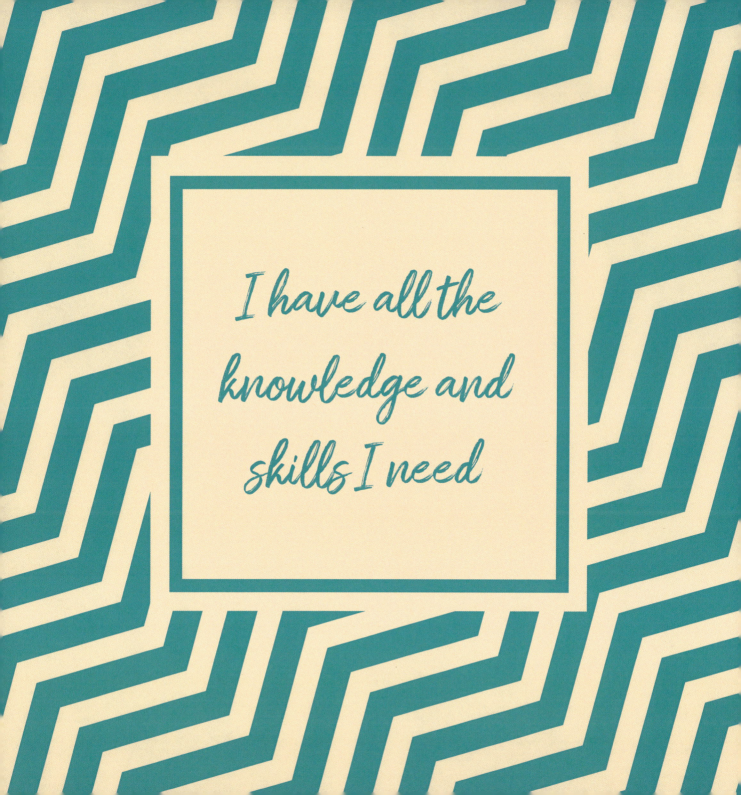

I have all the
knowledge and
skills I need

I treat my patients with dignity and respect

I choose to help
the sick because
I care deeply

I remember to care for myself as well as others

I become stronger after every storm

I can always find the good in other people even in trying times

I choose calm

over anxiety

I am efficient,
I am effective,
I am professional

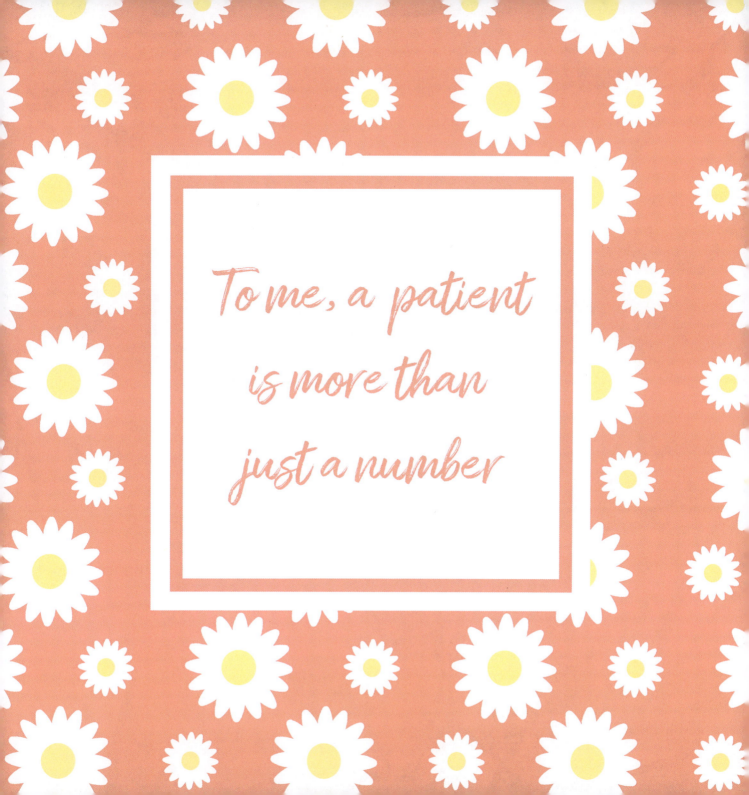

To me, a patient is more than just a number

I have the training and experience to face any situation

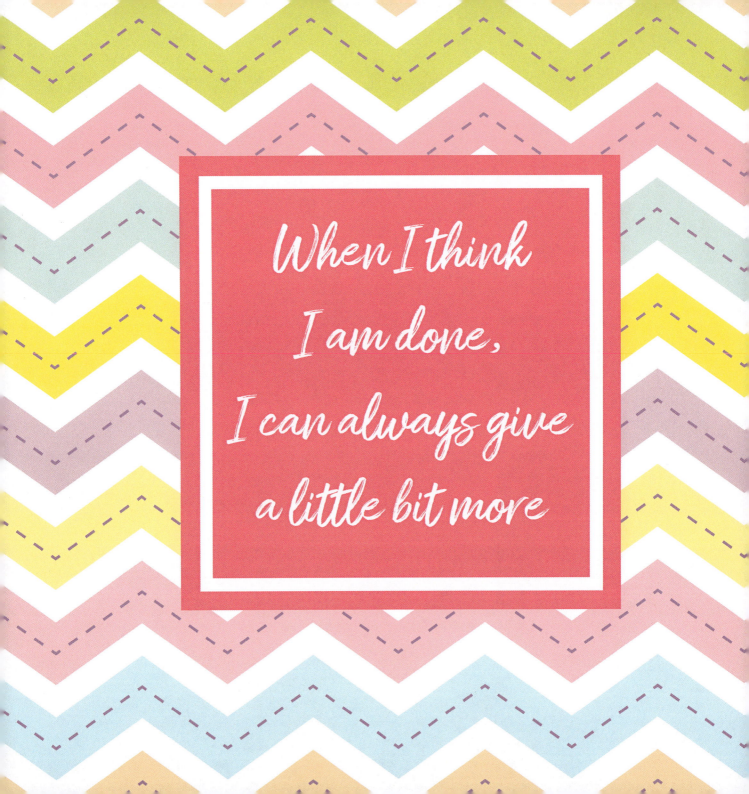

When I think
I am done,
I can always give
a little bit more

I can
and I will

I am calm
and controlled

in a crisis

I am supported by my colleagues every day

I forgive myself
for my mistakes

I feel my uncomfortable feelings then let them go

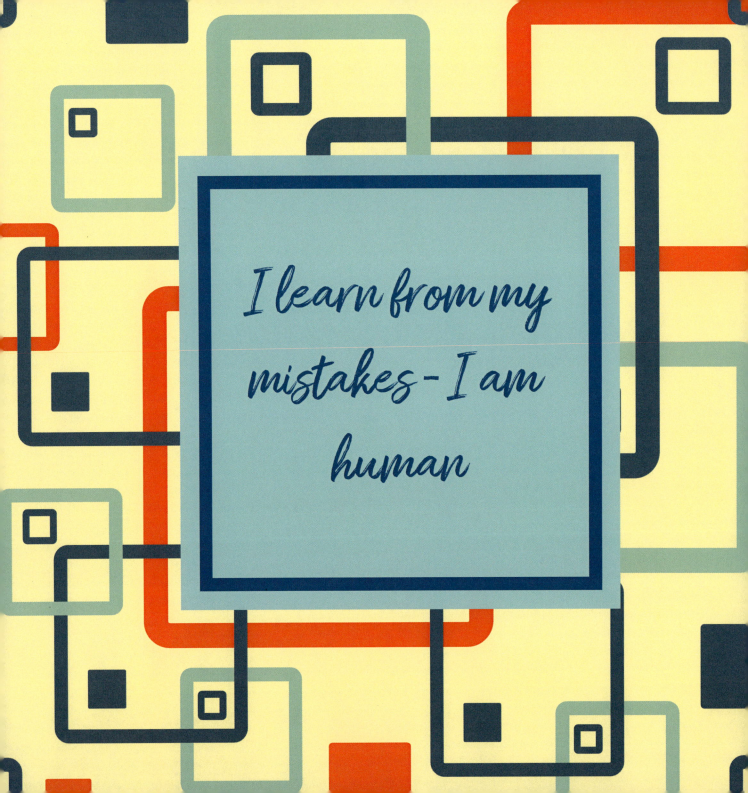

I learn from my mistakes - I am human

I make the world a better place

Today
I am ready for

anything

I am
a good nurse

I have empathy
for my patients

I have healthy boundaries with my patients and colleagues

I fearlessly tackle working outside of my comfort zone

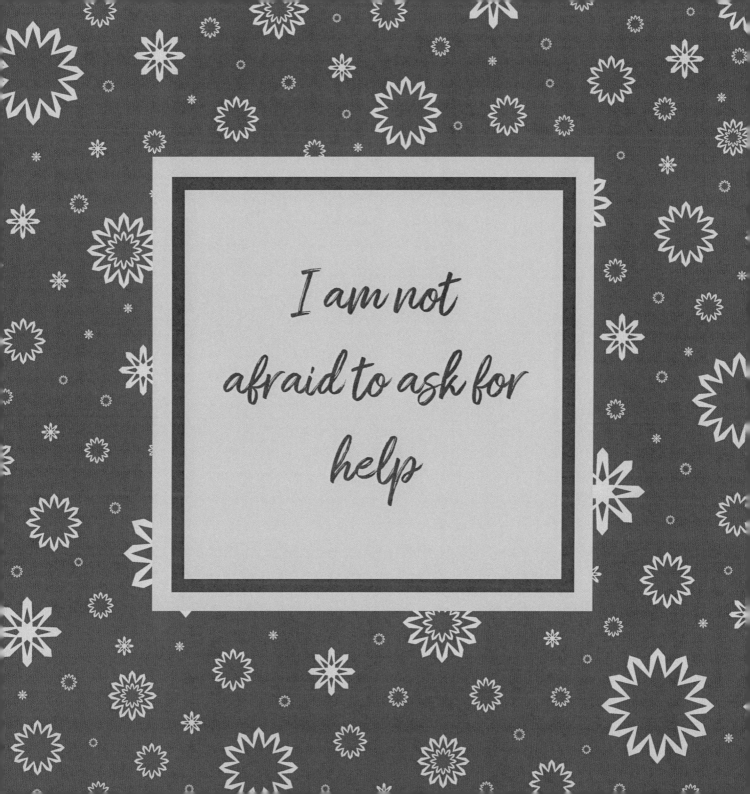

I am not afraid to ask for help

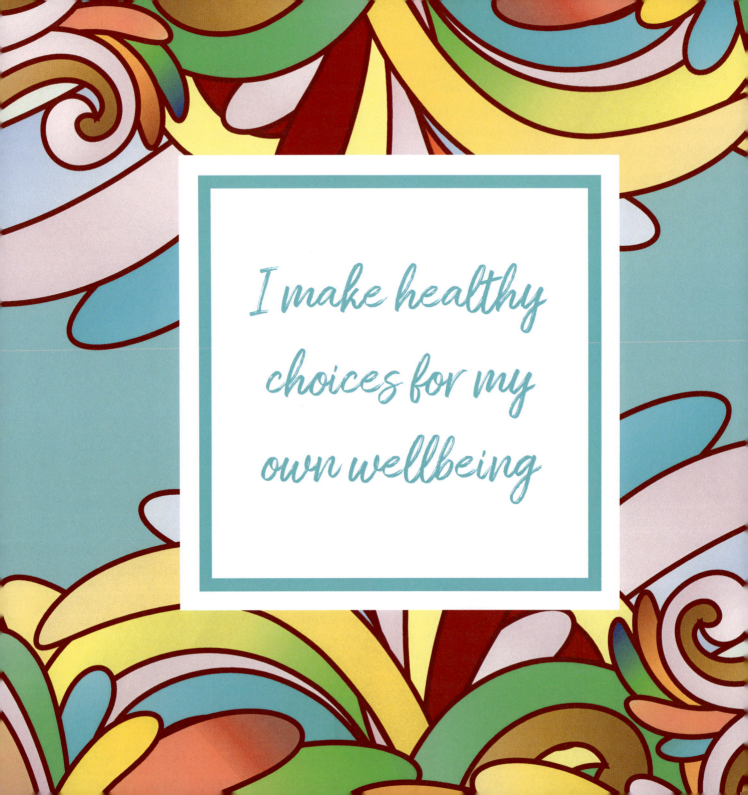

I make healthy choices for my own wellbeing

I am priveliged
I get to help those
in need

I choose to be present with my patients today

I cannot control
how others behave,
only the way
I react

Today I am

emanating

love and joy

I have patience
for all my
patients

I am kind to everyone I encounter every day

I choose to
eat good food
today to keep
my body healthy

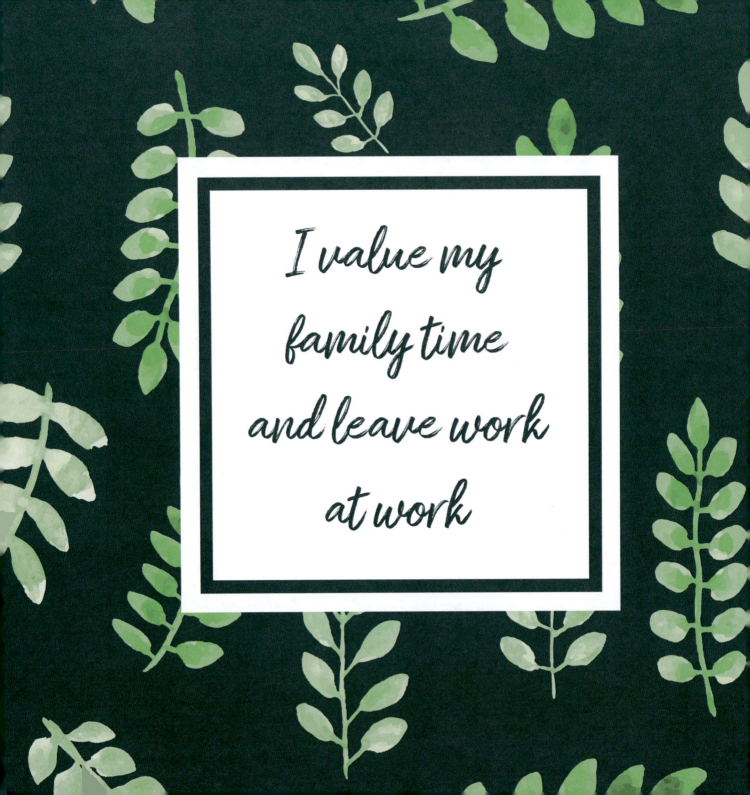

I value my family time and leave work at work

I trust my ability to make important decisions

I can solve
any problem I am
faced with

I listen to
my patients'
needs and do
everything I can

I focus on the things that I can change

I let go of
that which does
not serve me

I thrive when I am helping people

I support my co-workers in tough times

I encourage my patients to make good choices

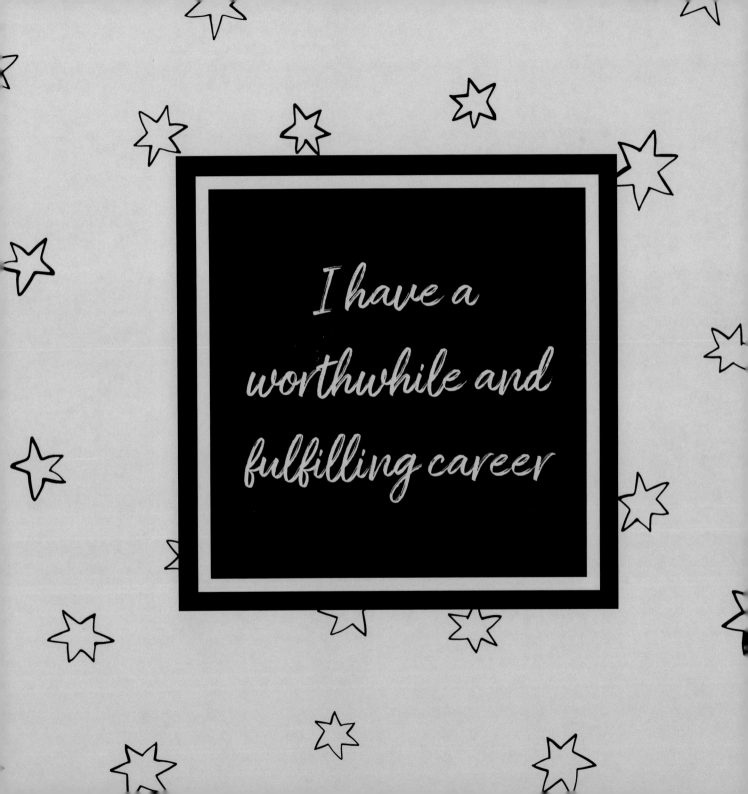

I have a worthwhile and fulfilling career

I am confident
in my abilities

I am stronger
than I know

I have the courage to show up each day

I embrace
what each new
day brings

I learn something from each new person I meet

I find the good
in any situation

I am the
rainbow in
someone's day

I am a valuable asset to my team

I trust my intuition

I choose to speak with confidence

I give my full attention to every task I undertake

I am kind to myself in times of uncertainty

Made in the USA
Monee, IL
13 April 2025

15694339R00038